W9-BED-663

37653011569996
McMath NonFiction
745.5941 NORDEN
Wedding details

AUG   2003

CENTRAL ARKANSAS LIBRARY SYSTEM
SIDNEY S. McMATH BRANCH LIBRARY
LITTLE ROCK, ARKANSAS

wedding details

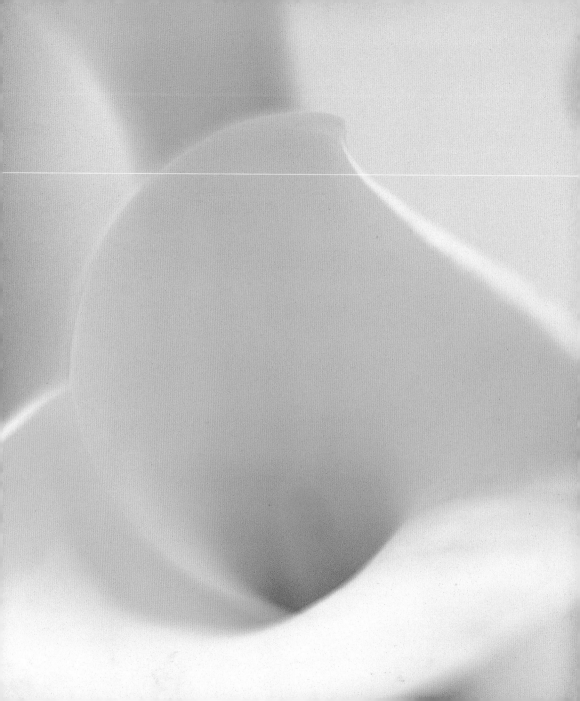

wedding details

mary norden

photography by polly wreford

HarperCollins*Publishers*
www.harpercollins.com

This book is dedicated to all brides to be.

Designer Catherine Randy
Senior editor Annabel Morgan
Editor Sophie Bevan
Location research manager Kate Brunt
Production Patricia Harrington
Publishing director Alison Starling
Art director Gabriella Le Grazie

Stylist Mary Norden

First published in Great Britain in 2000 by
Ryland Peters & Small

WEDDING DETAILS
Text copyright © 2000 Mary Norden
Design and photographs copyright © 2000 Ryland Peters & Small

3 5 7 9 10 8 6 4

All rights reserved. No part of this publication may be reproduced in
whole or in part or stored in a retrieval system, or transmitted in any
form or by any means, electronic, mechanical, photocopying,
recording, or otherwise without written permission of the publisher.
For information regarding permission, write to HarperCollins,
10 East 53rd Street, New York, NY 10022.

Library of Congress Cataloging-in-Publication Data
available on request
ISBN 0-688-17430-2

Printed and bound in China.

⟨library stamp, illegible⟩

contents

CENTRAL ARKANSAS LIBRARY SYSTEM
SIDNEY S. McMATH BRANCH LIBRARY
LITTLE ROCK, ARKANSAS

introduction

*W*eddings are not always the exclusive preserve of professionals. Many brides take great pleasure in choosing and arranging flowers, wrapping small tokens for guests to take home, and deciding on, or even making, the perfect gift to say thank you to the best man, maid of honor, and bridesmaids.

In these pages you'll find ideas for everything from setting the table for the wedding banquet to choosing the flowers for the bouquet. You'll see how simple wrapping can transform modest but thoughtful wedding favors into desirable packages, and discover novel ways to turn wedding ephemera like pressed flowers into exquisite keepsakes.

Every taste is catered to. From the cooly contemporary to the steadfastly traditional, you will find ideas that appeal and are sure to be inspired to add a few of your own.

classic wedding

The classic elegance of the white rose provided the inspiration for this stylish and traditional celebration. The creamy-white color theme was carried throughout, enlivened with touches of glossy green foliage for contrast and flashes of gilt to enhance the sophisticated effect.

Above and top: Each place setting includes an intriguing gift box, plus a white rose to echo the centerpieces and overall wedding theme.

Right: At the wedding table, all-white china can be a little severe. Add touches of pattern here and there, like the decorative foliage borders on these soup dishes. Starched white damask napkins folded into a triangle and rolled up, provide a neat fold for a placecard to be slipped inside.

Don't make your guests lean around flowers
to chat across the table. Instead, choose
low-level conversation-friendly centerpieces.

Crisp starched napkins are both beautiful and practical.
Fold them to hold breadsticks for each place setting to
serve with soup. By using plain white napkins you
repeat the chosen color theme, and a sprig of foliage
tucked into the folds adds contrast.

For the centerpiece, use a wreath of florist's oasis,
hidden with foliage and scattered with a few white
roses. Don't be too lavish with the roses. Err on

The frothy foliage and sophisticated lime-green flowers of bupleurum provide contrast and link different areas of the table setting. Tiny sprigs are arranged randomly against the pristine icing of the wedding cake (above) and tucked into napkins (far left), while longer stems are a perfect foil for the flawless white roses of the centerpiece (left).

Both contrasting and harmonizing
elements keep a classic theme going
successfully, from the wide white satin
bows used to decorate the dining
chairs (right), to the pattern of heavy
silverware (below) and the delicate
designs on the china (bottom).

the side of caution to maintain a
simple yet classic style.

To add an element of surprise
to the decorative theme of the
wedding tables, why not serve
one of the courses on patterned
china? Don't worry if you don't
have enough plates or bowls of
one design to serve all your
guests; simply use a different
pattern for each table.

You can also add touches of
color and texture in a variety of
unexpected ways—heavy antique
silverware with an embossed
pattern, for example, or the
contrasting ribbon used to fasten
the ribbed gift boxes.

The boxes here have been tied with two types of ribbon, layered one on top of the other. A plain green satin ribbon is topped with a length of dainty braid in lime green, picking up the color contrast between the leaves and flowers of the bupleurum sprigs scattered about the tables.

The details on the bridal gown—even the toe or heel of a slipper—can reflect the spirit of the whole day.

Above and right: Every bride should have the outfit of her dreams. From a border encrusted with beads to the elegantly embroidered columns of the bride's slippers, not a single detail should be overlooked. Delicate beading, buttons, and embroidery are all ways of adding style without being ostentatious. Using self-colored thread, beads, and buttons adds opulence while being discreet.

Left and above: Dress the bridesmaids to provide a beautiful backdrop for the bride. These shades of coffee-colored taffeta will complement the bridal gown perfectly. A big silk flower slipped into the sash looks suitably extravagant and is much more robust than the real thing. Save real roses for the bridesmaids' bouquets.

17

table settings

The table is the place where guests will probably spend much of their time, especially at a formal wedding breakfast or dinner. Although setting the table is likely to be the last of your tasks, it creates a vital first impression as people arrive. Making an effort to create original ideas for placecards, napkins, and flowers is time well spent. Buffet tables, too, offer plenty of scope for decoration.

napkins

Napkins are vital to protect delicate dresses and stylish suits from splashes and spills, but they also give you an opportunity to use your imagination when deciding how to present them. Choosing the very best quality napkins will add simple elegance to place settings, and—whether you go for fine linen tightly rolled, starched damask folded to form a fan, or gauzy organza dropped over a wine glass like a fallen parachute—to be really useful, the napkin should be generous in size. Accessories and trimmings should be simple but striking, such as garden greenery and lengths of ribbon.

Above: The original folds of this sheer organza add substance to the shape. Candied almonds complete the look.
Right: Starched damask is coaxed into pleats, then nipped in at the center with ribbon and a simple spray.

Left: To make these napkin rings, cut wide satin ribbon into 8-inch lengths. Write names on paper that is not too heavy; cut them out, and attach to the ribbon with spray glue. Wrap each length around a napkin and secure with glue or double-sided tape. Adding a sprig of rosemary not only looks decorative, it smells divine. **Above:** A single flower laid on a folded napkin adds instant elegance with precious little preparation.

21

Welcome friends and family to the wedding banquet: a well-laid table not only looks inviting, but makes your guests feel special.

This page: A starched damask napkin has been cleverly folded so a placecard can be neatly slipped under the top fold, while a single scabious *(Scabiosa)* flower makes a simple adornment.
Opposite: Silverware rolled in a napkin ready for a buffet and tied with a simple twist of ribbon is casual, yet stylish.

23

placecards

Novel ideas for placecards aren't hard to come up with. If you have a little time to spare, you can make some witty and unusual pointers to direct guests to their seats. For a lavish wedding, you might use a labeled favor. At a more relaxed event, chocolate name flags are good fun. You can either print names on a computer or write them neatly yourself. A classic italic script suits a formal wedding: it's easy to read with just a hint of a flourish. More ornate scripts can be difficult to decipher.

Left: To make these chocolate name flags, cut short lengths of wire-edged ribbon. Cut a fishtail at one end and attach double-sided tape to the other. Place a cocktail stick on the tape and roll inward to secure. Then cut the names into rectangles, glue each one onto a ribbon, and push the cocktail stick into a chocolate bonbon for a base.

This page and center: Placecards can be as lavish or as effortless as you want them to be. Set a wrapped favor at each place setting and use the label as a placecard, or simply stand a handwritten card in a beautiful cup and saucer.

Camilla

Xavier

Far left: Cupcake cases filled with glossy berries add a touch of vivid color to an all-white table setting. A handwritten placecard has been casually slipped in.

Center: Half a lemon is wrapped in pristine white cheesecloth and tied with white cotton tape to which a placecard is attached, ideal if you are serving a dish that needs lemon.

Right: A tiny bunch of trimmed asparagus is tied with satin ribbon threaded through a placecard and perched on top of each glass.

centerpieces

A table needs a focal point, and flowers have always been the conventional choice. For something just a bit different, arrangements of candles or extravagantly presented food can look striking, too. Take into account the formality of the occasion and the style of the menu being served, and choose a centerpiece accordingly. For a round table, a single centerpiece is ideal. On a long narrow table, you may want to repeat a series of arrangements down its length.

Glass cakestands come in many designs, from the ornately frilly to the severely classical, and can be used in the center of the table to hold all sorts of candy, cookies, and fruit, not just cake. Candles, too, make beautiful centerpieces. Thick altar candles running the entire length of the table or an arrangement of floating

Above: Narcissus flowers are tucked between frosted lemons in a glass compote.
Center left: An enticing array of petit-fours on a two-tier stand, made by simply standing a small dish on top of a larger one.

Center right: A bell-shaped Italian cake presented on a silver tray and tied with white ribbon makes an unusual centerpiece.
Opposite: White and silver candied almonds fill a Victorian fluted glass dish.

candles will bring a fairytale charm to the setting. Alternatively, you could choose the soothing flicker of decorated votive candles or a radiant display of tapers. But bear in mind that fancy designs and strident colors are out of place on an elegantly set table. For maximum impact, restrict your choice to white or ivory candles and plain column shapes to enhance the overall effect.

Far left: This strikingly
patterned bowl filled with
white roses makes a
sumptuous centerpiece. The
pink-and-white theme can
be repeated throughout
the table with pink napkins
and favor boxes tied with
matching pink ribbon.
Left: Glass desert bowls
each hold a single orchid
and combine with candles
to form an exotic display.
Above: A delicate china
cakestand holds a thick
altar candle surrounded by
a carpet of rose petals and
scattered narcissus flowers.

31

Conjure an air of romance and intimacy with a display of twinkling candlelight.

Above and left: Surround and emphasize a central vase with elegantly trimmed votives. Simply attach narrow pleated ribbon to the metal holders with double-sided tape.

Opposite: Tiny candles set afloat on a sea of scented rose petals make a luminous centerpiece at twilight.

Above: A handful of tapers stand in a white china bowl filled with a wedge of soaked florist's oasis to hold the candles in place and frothing with greenish-white cow parsley and sophisticated white Nerine. Tapers burn quickly, so aim to light them later in the meal, perhaps to celebrate speeches or toasts.

33

chair backs

Chair backs offer extra potential for decorating a room and have been relatively underused until recently. There is something very charming and quite unexpected about a chair embellished with a tied posy or trimmed with a big gauzy ribbon. Pay special attention to the bride's and groom's chairs, and use simpler ideas for the rest of the seating, if you prefer. Choose long-lasting flowers that will look good all day.

Hydrangeas are a good option as their papery flowers last well.

Left: A simple paper cone overflows with green and white variegated foliage and a froth of humble cow parsley tied with wide satin ribbon.
Above: A single diaphanous bow of palest yellow organdy softens this painted chair back.
Right: The washed-out sky blue of a mophead hydrangea is partnered with a narrow pale blue ribbon on a white bentwood chair.

Remember to fasten ribbons tightly so
they don't slip to one side or, worse,
lose their posies.

35

Fine accessories for the wedding table: a bone china coffee cup with a subtle handpainted gold scroll design (top); silver forks with pearly handles and embossed shanks (above); dinner plates with striking colored borders (right), and a row of elegant silver-topped salt shakers (far right).

table accessories

People eat with their eyes first, so presentation at the table is as important as the food that is served. Plain plates with a colored border frame food elegantly, while the shiniest, sparkliest glasses do justice to the wines offered. As with all very special occasions, it pays to be extravagant to achieve the effect you want. A well-orchestrated table reflects the special day, and quality really stands out—fine table linens, real silverware, crystal glasses, and bone-china coffee cups are unmistakable.

cakes

The cake can set the tone of the whole wedding. A classic tiered cake finished in smooth white icing is a blank canvas waiting to be decorated, so let your inspiration flow. Instead of getting all tangled up with complicated loops and swirls of conventional piped icing, a fresher and more contemporary look can be achieved by using ribbons and real flowers. For a winter wedding, when appropriate flowers can be scarce, a simple scattering of velvet blossoms is pretty and informal, while skeins of ivy would look darkly dramatic. In the fall, dahlias and wild berries would make bold and bright decorations.

A tiered, iced wedding cake is treated in three different ways, yet retains an overall simplicity of style.
Left: A generous trail of gauzy ribbon and a random sprinkling of pale pastel velvet flowers provide an effortlessly pretty look.

Above: A glamorous single rose is the ultimate in understated elegance.
Right: Broad bands of ribbon, an exotic orchid, and a few scattered silver and white candied almonds combine for a stylish, sophisticated cake.

contemporary
wedding

A contemporary wedding utilizes modern elements, but doesn't dispense with tradition altogether. Here classic white is combined with bold green to achieve the desired look. Striking sculptural flowers, unusual grasses, streamlined glassware, and simple white china all contribute to the overall effect.

The color scheme for this contemporary wedding still makes use of classic white, but the main impression is created by strongly contrasting green—and the way in which the colors have been combined makes it unmistakably modern. Green is an ideal theme for contemporary weddings, especially during the winter months, when fresh flowers are scarce and prices rise accordingly. Exotic flowers and grasses are widely available even in the depths of winter, as they are flown in from tropical climates. Here, they create a very different and original look, reinforced by the modern table setting where everything is streamlined and simple.

Above: Bold napkin rings can be made from flat glossy leaves rolled around napkins and tied in place with a few flexible grass stems.

Opposite: There is no distracting tablecloth, and all the glassware and china has clean graphic lines, from the cylindrical salt and pepper shakers to the alternating frosted-glass vases and candleholders.

43

Left: The tropical painter's palette flower *(Anthurium)* has a bold sculptural shape complemented by the exuberant fountains of bear grass *(Dasylirion)*. Although both are green in color, they couldn't be more different in form and texture.

Left and opposite: Pliable grass can be used instead of ribbon to tie favors or to hold a rolled-up menu. Use several strands of different shades of green for contrast. Here the menus have been printed on thick tracing paper, but parchment paper would work well, too.

Left: Small succulent plants like sedum or echeveria can be potted in decorative containers for alternative table arrangements. Spray small terracotta pots with silver paint (two thin coats are better than one thick one). When dry, plant up and finish with a silver ribbon. These would also make pretty and long-lasting mementoes for guests to take home.

Keep flower arrangements simple. Just a few well-chosen
blooms carefully presented make an exquisite
centerpiece for a contemporary table setting.

Far left: The pure clean lines of arum lilies *(Zantedeschia aethiopica)* are breathtaking in their simplicity. Flowers such as these and painter's palettes, both of which have strong outlines, create maximum impact arranged alone or with an absolute minimum of added foliage. Their strong graphic shapes make them especially suitable for modern, minimalist interiors.

Left: Waiters in simple, informal dress suit a wedding reception in a contemporary setting.

flowers

As soon as the date is set, check which flowers will be in season. There are good reasons for sticking to seasonal blooms: not only will costs be lower, but the flowers will also be more robust if they are at their peak. Let the bride's and bridesmaids' dresses guide you when choosing flower colors. Today, anything goes—from traditional white or cream to pink, apricot, or even bold red and purple.

bouquets

After the bride's gown, the flowers the bride carries are the next most important consideration. The bouquet's composition, color, and shape will set the tone for all the other flowers needed for the day.

Thankfully, rules of etiquette for wedding flowers have long been ignored. What matters is what you want—flowers should reflect your taste, plus the season and the style of the occasion. The bouquet can be an elaborate florist's arrangement or a simple posy gathered from your own backyard on the morning of the wedding. It may use flowers in tones that reflect the color of the gown or be a wild cascade of fiery colors for extra drama.

Left: A single orchid stem makes a dramatic statement.
Right: A handful of old-fashioned garden roses create a sweetly scented and romantic bouquet.

Left: Three flawless arum lilies, loosely tied, make a minimalist bouquet, perfect for a simple silk gown and a contemporary setting. For maximum drama, one single lily could be carried. **Right and above:** The polar opposite of pure white flowers—an unusual bouquet in shades of tawny orange and red. The orchids here are spotted with red that echoes the sprays of tiny red berries, and the stems are tied with a more traditional cream satin ribbon.

The simplest fragrant
handful tied with a
ribbon brings an extra
touch of romance to the
bride's outfit.

Opposite: When choosing flowers for a bouquet, aim to capture the season as well as the style and atmosphere of the wedding. Here a simple bunch of white longi lillies *(Lilium longiflorum)* mixed with sprays of white loosestrife *(Lysimachia clethroides)* has an air of summer elegance.
This page: The softest, dreamiest, and palest flowers are often a bride's first choice. This loosely tied posy of full-blown, creamy white ranunculus is subtle in color and romantic in style.

boutonnieres

Boutonnieres have come a long way since the obligatory carnation on a pin. With a little imagination, it's possible to fashion one from almost any plant. Flowers aren't vital—a spray of greenery can look equally stylish, and most backyards will yield a surprising selection, from rosemary to ivy or lilac. For a formal wedding, a rose beautifully dressed with a satin ribbon is the romantic's choice, while for a relaxed country occasion, a sprig of lime-green lady's mantle *(Alchemilla mollis)* looks charming. Whatever you choose, remove any thorns and wrap stems in florist's tape before binding with ribbon and adding a simple bow.

From left: Sprigs of white lilac *(Syringa)* with ribbon and braid; bold, variegated ivy with contrasting purple ribbon; rosemary sprigs—with or without flowers—are an aromatic choice; kangaroo paw *(Anigozanthos)* has long-lasting flower trumpets.
Right: A spray of white-flowered viburnum—a popular garden shrub—wrapped in ribbon for a delicate boutonniere.

table flowers

The most effective table arrangements are created by limiting the types of flowers to two or three species—or even just one. Simple themes are the easiest to put together and also the most inexpensive. Containers are important, too, and should be chosen to suit the flowers. Elegant lilies need a streamlined vase, while informal cottage-garden posies could be presented in containers concealed by rustic baskets. Remember to keep all arrangements low for uninterrupted cross-table talk.

Far left: A series of individual arrangements can be used to decorate the table; here a single orchid flower floats in a Victorian glass dessert dish.

Center: Flat scabious heads packed tightly into a glass vase make a satisfyingly rounded dome of flowers.

Left: A soup tureen is just the right height for a central arrangement of soft, papery hydrangea heads spiked with pink blooms of double lisianthus (*Eustoma grandiflorum*).

59

Fill shiny pails with a mass of frothy variegated foliage and a lacy topping of dill flowers.

Opposite and below: Miniature galvanized buckets are ideal for individual arrangements. Line them with one or two layers of white tissue paper, then add a layer of thin plastic sheeting and use soaked florist's foam

to hold the flowers and foliage. Trim any plastic that shows before setting them on the table.

Left: A small terracotta pot painted silver and filled with coordinated gray-green foliage and silvery-blue thistles, held in place using florist's foam.

The finished effect, using a large central arrangement echoed by individual ones at each place setting. These tiny galvanized buckets are hard to beat as flower containers: they're inexpensive, stylish, and their shiny finish suits a cream and green color scheme. The combination of variegated foliage and greenish-white flowers is imaginative and sophisticated.

floral wedding

Flowers are a focal point at an intimate wedding for family and
close friends. Working on a small scale gives you the opportunity
to be lavish with flowers. The blooms used here—paper-white
narcissi and indigo hyacinths—are modest enough flowers, but
massing them together looks extravagant.

The blue dining room at this wedding venue made easy work of deciding a color scheme. A timeless mix of blue and cream is emphasized with pale blue linen napkins, creamy white china and tablecloths, and a combination of similarly colored flowers. The overall effect is charming and effortless—the ideal atmosphere for a low-key, relaxed wedding. If you have time to plan ahead, instead of using cut flowers, plant pots with bulbs and coax them into bloom in time by bringing them in from the cold a few weeks before the wedding.

Left: The table is set with terracotta flower pots painted white and brimming over with a heady mix of narcissi and hyacinths. The flowers are arranged in glass jars, hidden from view inside the pots.

Far left: Unfussy folded napkins and plain china and glassware set the tone for a small gathering of family and friends.
Above: A humble wooden bench spruced up with a coat of paint makes an informal dining-room seat.

67

Continue the color theme throughout the house or venue with the use of generous bows and carefully placed arrangements.

Left and right: Large bunches of narcissi or daffodils look wonderful on their own. Put them into a big container, and you have a simple arrangement in an instant. Old-fashioned enamel pails are ideal, in classic white with navy blue trim or a more unusual shade of pale blue. Stand them casually at the foot of the stairs or by the door. **Top**: An alternative way to present the napkins, tied with gingham bows.

favors

Favors need not be elaborate or expensive. The best are often simple gifts, imaginatively wrapped and presented. Send your guests home with memories of a very special day and a tiny memento to say thank you for coming—you'll be following a tradition that can be traced back to ancient Rome.

edible

Favors based on candy and food are always popular. Dragees— almonds in a sugar coating—are traditional wedding favors: the nuts symbolize fertility as they are the seeds of the almond tree, and the combination of bitter almonds and sweet coating represents the "for better and for worse" part of the wedding vows. Homemade cookies, chocolates, packages of nuts, and even fruit can all be given as mementoes. The perfect time to serve edible favors is with after-dinner coffee—though you then run the risk that they may not last long enough to be taken home.

Right: Small chocolate-filled bags are folded from matte gold paper, tied with cream organza and satin ribbon, and finished with a beaded berry.
Opposite: Cellophane cones are filled with white jelly beans and tied with a flourish of mint-green ribbon.

Fitting mementoes of a special day—edible wedding favors need to be not only delicious, but beautifully dressed, too.

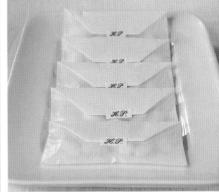

Above and left: Glassine bags—the semiopaque paper envelopes used to protect photographic negatives and transparencies—make ideal wrappings for favors. Here they have been lined with an additional layer of lacy Japanese paper and filled with candied almonds. The finishing touch is a snippet of name tape embroidered with the couple's initials and used to seal the bag.

Far left: White bonbons make a pretty alternative to candied almonds. To wrap, cut circles of cellophane, place a handful in the center, bring up the edges, and tie with ribbon. You could also wrap them in circles of dressmaker's net or tulle, but leave the cellophane layer in place to stop powdered sugar from leaking.

The easiest way to give every guest a piece of wedding cake is to box slices for them to take home. Cartons are sold ready-made for the purpose—just pile the filled boxes on an antique serving platter placed near the door so guests can help themselves as they leave. Here, clusters of snowberries *(Symphoricarpos)* have been tucked between the boxes for decoration.

nonedible

A favor can be as simple as a bundle of candles or handful of spring bulbs
to plant at home: it's the novelty of the gift that makes it memorable.
Packaging doesn't have to be elaborate; it can be simple but still look
stylish. Glassine bags are ideal for loose items, while boxes make awkwardly
shaped gifts neater and easier to handle. At an Easter wedding, a
hollowed egg handpainted with the initials of the bride and groom would
make a simple but unusual parting gift.

Far left: Bundles of thin
hand-dipped candles
secured with satin cord and
presented to guests on a
silver platter make novel
favors to take home.
Center left: Boxes of
delicately corrugated
cardboard can be used to
hold spring or summer
bulbs for a long-lasting
memento.
Left: Glassine bags used to
wrap bars of extra-special
scented soap. Use a hole
punch to perforate the top
of the bag, fold it over, and
thread ribbon through the
hole to secure.

79

Plain white paper bags filled with loose tea make charming wedding favors to take home. Choose an out-of-the-ordinary blend or something exotic. Fold down the bags to resemble a rectangular envelope and fasten with narrow ribbon. Arrange the favors in neat rows along bands of wide satin ribbon (inset) or pile them casually under a vase of flowers on a hall table or sideboard (main picture).

Wedding favors express your gratitude and serve to remind friends and family of their participation in the wedding.

Left: Sometimes the packaging is as important as the contents. These favor boxes may hold cookies, soaps, or miniature scented candles. Whatever the contents, they are intriguingly embellished.

Above: Flower seeds repackaged in luxurious envelopes will bring results to be enjoyed long after the wedding is over.

Right: Special messages or photographs rolled in scrolls of tracing paper make very personal souvenirs of a wonderful day. Pile them in a glass dish and let guests help themselves.

romantic wedding

This location provided the inspiration for a truly romantic wedding. The walls are embellished with a discreet, delicate ribbon and flower motif and even the chairs are shapely and curvaceous. Thick damask cloths, fine bone china, filigreed glasses, and sugar-pink flowers carry the theme right through to the dining table.

Pink is a romantic, very feminine color and a favorite choice for bridesmaids' dresses and table settings. For pure romance, old-fashioned softer colors work best: think of the delicate shades of pale pink sweet peas and peonies. Some roses and tulips come in much hotter pinks for vibrant arrangements that will make a bolder statement. Use pink at the table for the flowers and repeat hints of the color in the wrapping for favors or ribbon-tied napkins. A table laid for an intimate wedding banquet, as shown here, could easily be scaled up to accommodate more guests at a larger wedding. Lots of small circular tables can be used to seat people

Above: The romantic details at the table include a glass compote full of ribbon-wrapped favors, an elegant carafe, and extravagant pink flowers. **Left:** Pink hydrangeas and double lisianthus are an unconventional but pretty choice for wedding flowers. Cutting the stems low creates a full, rounded arrangement that focuses attention on the flowers.

instead of one large table, and smaller chairs are an option if space around the tables becomes limited.

Little, unexpected touches can reinforce a theme with surprising emphasis. The curves and moldings of a pretty painted chair, a tablecloth that elegantly sweeps the floor—elements that say romance out loud. Make use of these and similar details throughout the dining room and wedding location to set the tone for the day.

Left: Chiffon bows tied to door handles, a tiny posy casually laid on a pushed back chair—if the details are perfect, everything will fall into place.

Above and right: Oyster-colored ribbon and a bloom flushed with pink complete each table setting.

Far right: The delicate pastels of the wall decoration inspired the choice of colors for the wedding flowers.

89

Not so long ago, the cake—like the
bride—could only be dressed in white.
But what could be more appropriate for a
romantic wedding than a blush of pink
icing and a shower of bright blossoms?

The tiered cake is set on its own table in the window, on a damask cloth to match that of the main table. Individual hydrangea flowerets have been used to decorate the cake—these could be saved and pressed between the pages of a book, then used to adorn thank-you cards and letters, to remind guests of the wedding flowers.

Many brides dream of a
truly romantic wedding
with a very feminine
emphasis. Seize every
opportunity to add as much
romance to the special day
as you can.

From left: Satin slingbacks
with extravagant feather
bows make fairytale bridal
slippers; antique
champagne flutes, etched
with romantic vines and
flowers, are served on a
precious silver tray; a
candle sconce garlanded
with crystal drops casts the
most flattering light of all.

finishing touches

Use these tiny but all-important details to personalize a wedding and

add your own indelible style to the day. Here you'll find ideas for confetti,

gifts for your bridesmaids and other important attendants, plus ring bags

and pillows. Some will involve a little sewing or advance preparation; others

are simply a question of presentation.

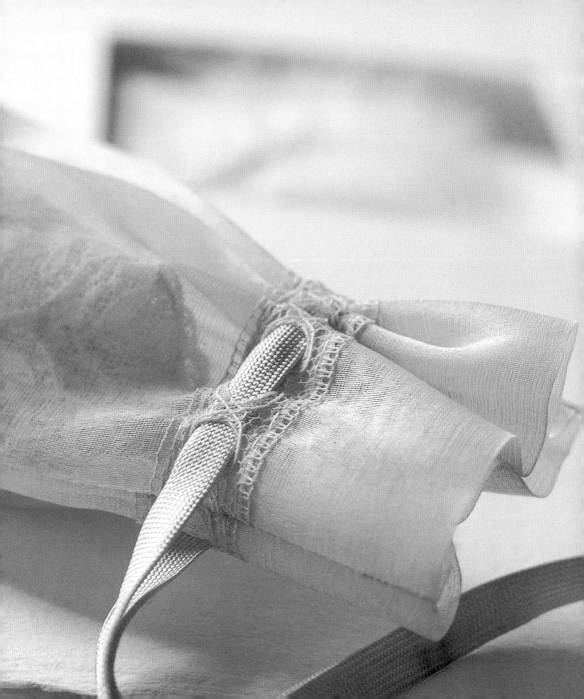

confetti

"Confetti" can be used instead of the more traditional option of rice to shower the bride and groom as they leave the ceremony. It's fun to make your own. Flower petals, rose petals in particular, are perhaps the most romantic choice. If you are picking flowers from your own backyard, cut them early on the morning of the wedding when they are at their freshest, so the petals will still look their best later in the day. If you need a large quantity of petals, eke them out by mixing them with colored tissue-paper shapes. Birdseed—another popular choice—looks best presented in pretty packages. Pile bags, cones, or boxes of confetti onto a large tray or into a basket and leave it by the door to the wedding venue, so each guest can pick up a package after the service.

Opposite: For an informal country wedding, an old enamel pail has been filled with freshly picked rose petals and tiny flower heads. The bucket can be passed around so that every guest can take a handful.

Above left and right: Cones of handmade paper make charming containers for confetti. Alternatively, fill small cardboard candy boxes with petals and tie with a ribbon until the contents are needed.

Always check beforehand that it is permitted to throw rice or petals—some places object to the debris left behind.

Parchment envelopes, simple
wooden boxes that strawberries
are sold in, even miniature
galvanized buckets—all these
can be used to hold "confetti".
Flower petals are the ultimate
biodegradable confetti, though they
won't disappear overnight—unlike
birdseed, which is guaranteed to.
Remember, too, that rice can be
harmful to birds if it is swallowed.

Far left: Glassine bags perforated with
a hole punch and secured with a twist
of raffia keep birdseed confetti from
spilling. These bags have been stacked
on a Chinese bamboo sifter—a shiny
silver tray or a shallow basket would
work well, too.
Left: A wicker basket normally used
for carrying wine bottles is ideal for
holding paper cones of confetti.

Top: A pleated pintucked silk satin ring bag tied with velvet ribbon.

Above: A ring pillow of textured wool, trimmed with silk picot edging and a central button.

Right and far right: An unusual stitched button or a Chinese bead make ideal fastenings for a ring bag.

ring bags and pillows

Don't let the best man go through the ritual of patting each pocket in turn
to find the rings. If you make a ring bag, he'll be able to tell immediately
where it is. All you need is a remnant or two of exquisite fabric—perhaps
left over from the bride's dress—plus an unusual bead or button and a scrap
of silk cord or ribbon. If you prefer, stitch a ring pillow for the page boy to
carry instead. Either way, you won't need a sewing machine—all these ideas
are simple to sew by hand.

gifts for attendants

The giving of presents to say thank you to attendants is an ancient tradition. It is easy to lose sight of what the day means to all those around you, so remember your maid of honor, bridesmaids, and flower girls with gifts to show how much you appreciate their participation. You may want to help the groom choose and wrap his presents to his best man and groomsmen, too. Gifts can range from the simplest embroidered hankies to grander offerings such as jewelry, or something very personal such as a first edition of a favorite book. Whatever you give, it should be an enduring memento of the day: this is one instance where edible gifts aren't really appropriate.

Above: A gift of tiny monogramed pillows filled with fragrant lavender.
Right: Take as much care in wrapping the gift as you did in buying it. Layers of ribbon and a velvet flower turn a package from functional to beautiful.

Above: If you give small pieces of jewelry such as cuff links or earrings, keep an eye open for unusual boxes like this 1930s pill box. Line it with tissue paper to hold the item, but there's no need to wrap it: it looks quite intriguing as it stands.

Left: Lavender sachets made from exquisitely embroidered linen can be awkward to wrap, so they are more easily packed in a candy box.

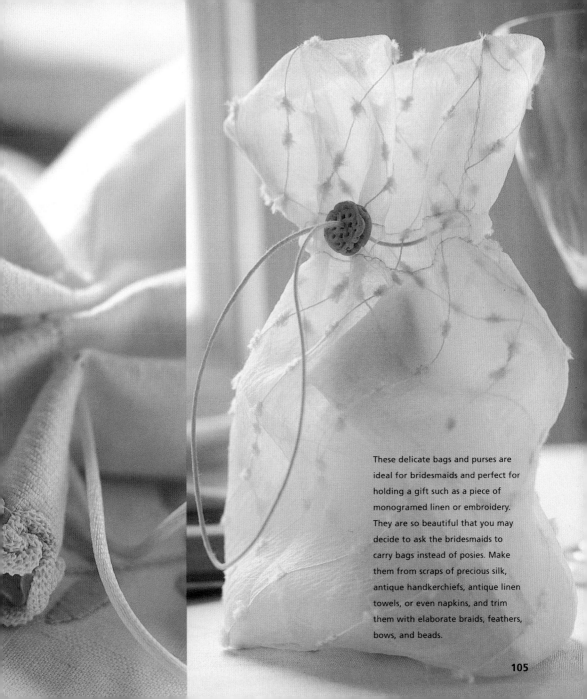

These delicate bags and purses are ideal for bridesmaids and perfect for holding a gift such as a piece of monogramed linen or embroidery. They are so beautiful that you may decide to ask the bridesmaids to carry bags instead of posies. Make them from scraps of precious silk, antique handkerchiefs, antique linen towels, or even napkins, and trim them with elaborate braids, feathers, bows, and beads.

Say thank-you in the most personal way. Indulge your bridesmaids and other attendants with gifts that can be used again and again.

Translucent mother-of-pearl boiled-egg spoons make exquisite gifts to say thank-you to wedding attendants. You could add an initialed egg cup to make the present complete. A pair of antique silver-lidded mother-of-pearl pepper and salt shakers would make an elegant alternative.

country wedding

An informal wedding followed by a reception in the community center is one of the most relaxed ways to celebrate a marriage. Despite the effortless appearance of the table and the food, careful planning is still essential to make the day a success. As always, the little details—the sweep of the checked cloth over the linen, the little bunches of lavender—are all important.

Wire baskets of bread, bottles of olive oil, and luscious figs set a table that is generous and bountiful. Sprigs of fresh lavender tied with lilac ribbon to decorate the napkins and informal arrangements of ranunculus and white loosestrife *(Lysimachia clethroides)* standing in large old-fashioned pitchers add to the relaxed atmosphere of the occasion.

111

This page: The elements of a rustic wedding: good bread laid straight onto the cloth as they would in France, rich fruity olive oil for dipping, and simple cottage-garden flowers.
Opposite: Dress all tables to match the buffet, with similar cloths and flowers.

If you cannot find colorful tablecloths to buy or rent, it's easy to make your own—and that way you'll get exactly what you want. A simple hem transforms a length of fabric into the tablecloth of your choice. Lay the patterned cloth over plain white linen and scoop it up in the center; secure the gathers with

a safety pin and add a bundle of lavender and a lilac satin bow to form a focal point.

When guests help themselves from a buffet, the majority will stand and eat. However, it's a good idea to have a few small tables dotted around the room for the people who prefer to sit down.

Have candles on hand as dusk falls.
Sheltering in storm lanterns or glass jars,
their soothing flickers cast a warm glow.

Far left: Modest wooden baskets hold a fragrant mix of rice and lavender confetti. Remember that rice should not be thrown where birds might eat it.
Center: Dress plain chairs to match the table, using two bunches of lavender tied end to end. Disguise the join with a lilac satin sash.
Above: These galvanized mesh storm lanterns light the way on the stairs. Place others at strategic points, on windowsills and tables, and outdoors, at gate posts and along paths.

keepsakes

Photographs are the most literal reminders of a happy day, but all sorts of objects can become treasured mementoes. There are bound to be keepsakes that you want to store safely alongside the photographs. Here are some ideas for keepsakes for the bride and groom, and to send to close friends and family.

Below: Send wedding pictures framed in a homemade card, folded in three so the front two flaps open like window shutters. Line them with tissue and add ribbons to fasten.

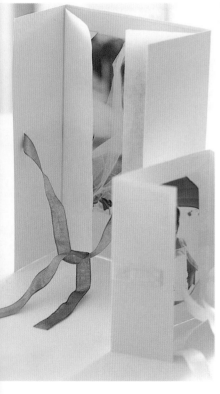

Careful storage of mementoes will mean that your wedding memories can last a lifetime. Photographs should be kept in complete darkness to prevent fading, and one way to store them safely is to make a wedding portfolio. This is a much more informal way of keeping and displaying photographs than a traditional heavy leather album. Add other treasured memories such as menus, sheet music, telegrams from absent friends and family, the notes from the best man's speech and the order of the service – anything that is important to you.

Above: To make a portfolio, bind two large pieces of cardboard together along the spine with cream-colored tape; tape across the corners, too, for extra protection as well as decoration. Make a slit on each outer edge and thread ribbon through, securing one end on the inside with a dab of glue or piece of tape.

Make thank-you cards using pressed leaves from the bouquet. Tear out three rectangles of thick artist's watercolor paper and fold in half. Stitch them together through the center, then tie with velvet cord and use spray glue to attach leaves to the pages.

Individual keepsake albums to send to
friends and family can be made from
thick artist's watercolor paper tied
with narrow ribbon. Cut a window in
the cover to reveal a photo, a tiny
pleated paper fan, a scrap of sheet
music, or buttons from the bride's or
bridesmaid's dresses.

Pressed flowers and leaves taken from the bride's

bouquet, scraps of fabric, exquisite trimmings,

even buttons, can all spark happy memories.

After the whirl of the day, you will be left with wonderful memories. Cherish every one of these with precious mementoes. A very personal and visual collection of keepsakes can be displayed on an artist's canvas stretched over a frame, as shown here. You could include buttons, cufflinks, squares of fabric, skeins of embroidery thread, special trimmings—such as lace, cord, and braid—earrings, buckles, and even tiny pockets of birdseed confetti. Include anything that holds special memories—it's entirely up to you.

Old-fashioned luggage tags have been used to frame and attach all sorts of trinkets, each hung from the string of the tag and secured with a pin.

123

sources

Ribbons and trimmings

Elliot, Greene & Company
37 West 37th Street
New York, NY 10018
Tel: 212-391-9075
Fax: 212-391-9079
Minimum order $25. They carry rhinestones, sequins, and beads of all description including some in glass, wood, plastic, and metal.

Hyman Hendler & Sons
67 West 38th Street
New York, NY 10018
Tel: 212-840-8393
Fax: 212-704-4237
Minimum order $50. Basic, novelty, and vintage ribbons.

Paul's Veil & Net Corp.
42 West 38th Street
New York, NY 10018
Tel: 212-391-3822
Net, nylon tulles, and silk illusions.

The Ribbonerie
191 Potrero Avenue
San Francisco, CA 94103
Tel: 415-626-6184
Website: www.theribbonerie.com
This store carries a range of both domestic and imported ribbons.

Cakes

Cherry Blossom Bakery
914 E Camelback Road
Phoenix, AZ 85014-3662
Tel: 602-248-9090

Creative Cakes
400 East 74th Street
New York, NY 10021
Tel: 212-794-9811

Phoenicia Bakery
3381 Adams Avenue
San Diego, CA 92116-1823
Tel: 619-282-1131

Candles

Illuminations
Mailing address:
1995 South McDowell Blvd.
Petaluma, CA 94954
Tel: 707-769-2700
and 800-CANDLES (226-3537)
Website: www.illuminations.com
An array of candles, candle accessories, and home-decor products.

Covington Candle
976 Lexington Avenue
New York, NY 10021
Tel: 212-472-1131
Fax: 212-717-8186
E-mail: covcandle@aol.com
Custom-made dinner and pillar candles in various colors and sizes, particularly more unusual and hard-to-find sizes.

Chandlers Candle Company
Tel: 530-621-1739
and 800-463-7143
Fax: 530-621-2154
E-mail: info@chandlerscandle.com
Website: www.chandlerscandle.com

Confetti
Exclusively Weddings
Dept bb40
1301 Caroline Street
Greensboro, NC 27401
Tel: 800-759-7666
Website:
www.exclusivelyweddings.com
Rose petals, seed, rice, and bubbles,
plus favors and gifts.

Rice Roses
2689 Caladium Drive
Atlanta, GA 30345
Tel: 800-240-9900
Fax: 770-939-5617
E-mail: jktn2@aol.com
Confetti.

ShindigZ.com
PO Box 86
Larwill, IN 46764
Tel: 877-446-3449
Website: www.ShindigZ.com
On-line bridal superstore.

Paper, cards, and stationery

Kate's Paperie
561 Broadway
New York, NY 10012
Tel: 212-941-9816
and 888-941-9169
E-mail: info@katespaperie.com
Website: www.katespaperie.com
Kate's Paperie carries over 40,000
exotic papers from around the world
as well as elegant gifts, unique
stationery, journals, photo albums,
and fine pens. Also on offer are
paper-related services including
custom printing and custom
gift-wrapping.

The Precious Collection
P.O. Box 100
Peosta, IA 52068-0100
Tel: 800-553-9080
Website: www.wedding.orders.com
Wedding invitations and accessories.

Now & Forever
P.O. Box 820
Goshen, CA 93227-0820
Tel: 800-451-8616
Wedding stationery and accessories.

The Written Word
1365 Connecticut Avenue NW
Washington, DC 20036
Tel: 202-223-1400
E-mail: writword@aol.com
Website:
www.writtenword.invitations.com
Specialists in handmade papers and
letterpress printing.

Favors and details

Carson Enterprises Inc.
630 Towne Square
Fairfield, OH 45014
Tel: 800-995-2288
Fax: 513-785-4794
Website: www.heresheis.com
Chocolate reception favors.

H&L Novelties Inc.
76 Dover
Trenton, NJ 08638
Tel: 609-882-3080
Customized matchbooks available in
various fragrances.

Wedding Cameras
6560 Latona Avenue NE
Seattle, WA 98115
Tel: 800-310-0464
Website: www.blard.net/~camsinc.
Single-use flash cameras to set on
tables.

General suppliers

Camelot Wedding Software
The Wedding Software Co.
For a retailer near you,
call 800-589-7333
Website:
www.bangzoom.com/camelot
Computer software that helps you
create guest lists, budgets, stationery,
envelopes, labels, and checklists.

Cathy's Concepts
For a retailer near you,
call 800-969-7417
Romantic bridal accessories and gifts.

Forever & Always Co.
110 West Manlius Street
East Syracuse, NY 13057
Tel: 800-404-4025
Website: www.foreverandalways.com
Candles, chocolates, guest books,
goblets, garters, novelty favors,
and more.

Marilyn's Keepsakes
P.O. Box 479
Fishers, IN 46038
Website: www.marilynkeepsakes.com
Engraved gifts and coordinated
wedding accessories.

WSI Product Network
210 C North 21st Street
Purcellville, VA 20132
Tel: 888-266-7438
Fax: 540-338-8165
E-mail: GoWSI@aol.com
Website: theweddingshopper.com
One-stop shopping wedding
superstore (everything but the dress).

Useful websites
www.weddingchannel.com
www.theknot.com
www.weddings.com

acknowledgments

My biggest thanks go to Polly Wreford for creating such evocative pictures and for her ability to remain so enthusiastic about so many weddings and to discover a fresh approach to each one. Thank you also to her assistant, Matt.

A special thank you to Kirsten Robinson, my assistant, for all her help with the deluge of props and for being the perfect bride. Thank you to Ella Ackroyd for giving up a day of her vacation to be such a beautiful bridesmaid.

I would like to thank Annabel Morgan, my wonderful editor, for all her support and love of weddings which was so contagious. Also, at Ryland Peters & Small, thank you to Alison Starling, Gabriella Le Grazie, Kate Brunt, and Catherine Randy. Thanks to my agent Fiona Lindsay of Limelight Management.

I am very grateful to the many people who kindly lent us their table linens, silverware, china, and glassware. I would like to thank Melanie Sauze for her exquisite sewing, and Jane Cassini and Sandra Lee for all their beautiful keepsakes.

My husband, as always, has been a constant support. Thank you, Charles.

The author and publisher would also like to thank everyone who allowed them to photograph in their homes, including Lena Proudlock (Denim in Style, Drews House, Leighterton, Gloucestershire GL8 8UN. Tel/Fax: 01666 890 230), Freddie Daniells, and Clare Pike.